hjbnf   HEB
522.6 AGUI

Aguilar, PORTER, author
Luna
33410015437207   08/14/19

W9-AEH-249

PORTER COUNTY
LIBRARY SYSTEM

Hebron Public Library
201 W. Sigler Street
Hebron, IN 46341

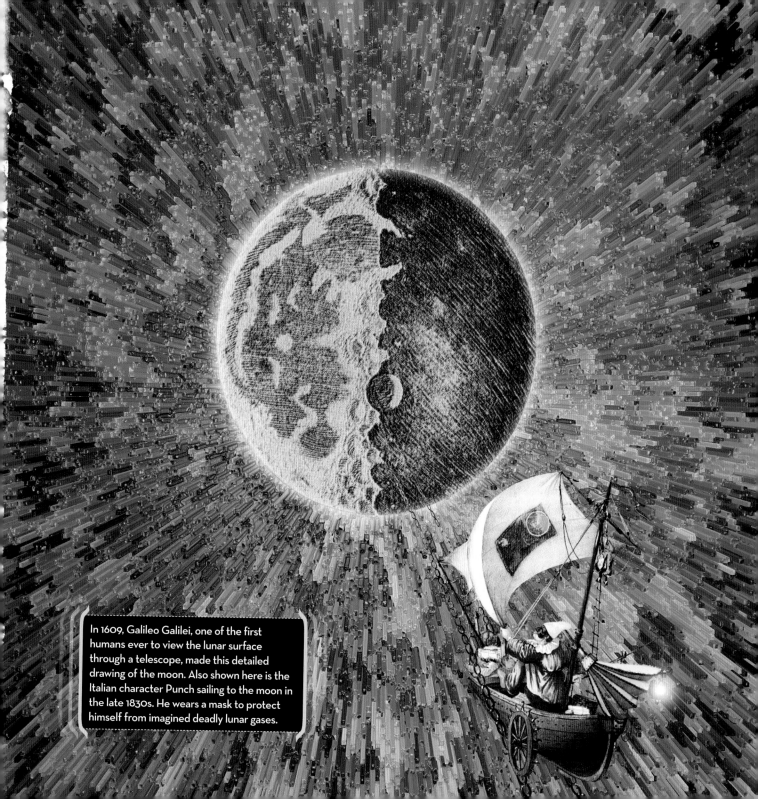

In 1609, Galileo Galilei, one of the first humans ever to view the lunar surface through a telescope, made this detailed drawing of the moon. Also shown here is the Italian character Punch sailing to the moon in the late 1830s. He wears a mask to protect himself from imagined deadly lunar gases.

NATIONAL
GEOGRAPHIC
KiDS

LUNA

The **SCIENCE** and **STORIES** of Our **MOON**

DAVID A. AGUILAR

NATIONAL GEOGRAPHIC
Washington, D.C.

CONTENTS

Created by author H.G. Wells in his 1901 book, *The First Men in the Moon*, Selenites are fictional, five-foot (1.5-m)-tall antlike creatures that inhabit tunnels beneath the surface of the moon.

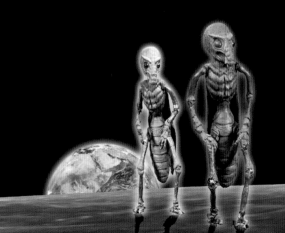

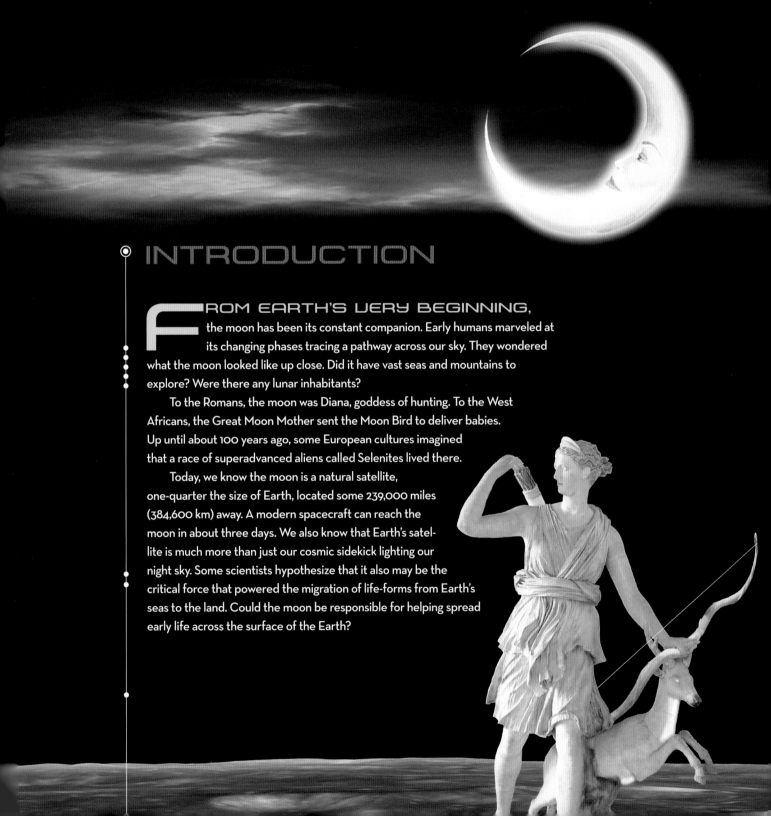

INTRODUCTION

FROM EARTH'S VERY BEGINNING, the moon has been its constant companion. Early humans marveled at its changing phases tracing a pathway across our sky. They wondered what the moon looked like up close. Did it have vast seas and mountains to explore? Were there any lunar inhabitants?

To the Romans, the moon was Diana, goddess of hunting. To the West Africans, the Great Moon Mother sent the Moon Bird to deliver babies. Up until about 100 years ago, some European cultures imagined that a race of superadvanced aliens called Selenites lived there.

Today, we know the moon is a natural satellite, one-quarter the size of Earth, located some 239,000 miles (384,600 km) away. A modern spacecraft can reach the moon in about three days. We also know that Earth's satellite is much more than just our cosmic sidekick lighting our night sky. Some scientists hypothesize that it also may be the critical force that powered the migration of life-forms from Earth's seas to the land. Could the moon be responsible for helping spread early life across the surface of the Earth?

"THAT'S ONE SMALL STEP FOR MAN, ONE GIANT LEAP FOR MANKIND ... The surface is fine and powdery. I can kick it up loosely with my toe. It does adhere in fine layers like powdered charcoal, to the sole and sides of my boots. I only go in a small fraction of an inch, maybe an eighth of an inch, but I can see the footprints of my boots and the treads in the fine, sandy particles."

—Neil Armstrong's first words while standing on the surface of the moon
July 20, 1969

"BEAUTIFUL, BEAUTIFUL ... MAGNIFICENT DESOLATION!"

—Buzz Aldrin's first words as the second person to step foot on the moon
July 20, 1969

Earth is always visible from the surface of the moon. Instead of following a pathway across the sky (like the moon seems to do from Earth), it hangs in one location. Like the moon in our sky, though, Earth does appear to slowly change phases.

FIRST STEPS
ON THE MOON

THE APOLLO PROGRAM SENT SEVEN LUNAR MIS-SIONS to the moon, where a total of 12 astronauts walked on the moon's surface. The NASA program, which began in 1961 and ended in 1972, included missions to collect lunar rock samples and conduct scientific experiments. Later missions included the lunar rover, which bumped across the rugged lunar landscape at about seven miles an hour (11 km/h).

The arrival of humans on the moon marked one of the most momentous scientific and engineering achievements in history. Those first footprints left by the Apollo astronauts will not last forever. But they will be there for a long, long time. With no atmosphere, there are no winds, rains, or floods to erode the moon's surface. There are no actively erupting volcanoes to alter its features.

However, its landscape is constantly bombarded by micro-meteorites half the size of a grain of salt. These tiny particles chip away at lunar rocks and slowly reshape the surface. But don't worry. You may still get to see those footprints in person—they won't be covered by dust or worn away completely for possibly 100 million years!

Though you may not be able to go to the moon today, we can still explore it together. Instead of flying in a lunar shuttle, we'll use Earth-based telescopes and our imaginations to explore the far side of the moon as well as the near side, with its rolling mountains and cavernous craters. We'll revisit some ancient legends that were used by earlier generations to explain lunar mysteries. In this book, you'll explore our marvelous moon and all the ways it affects your life from 239,000 miles (384,600 km) away.

COSMIC CHAOS

FOUR AND A HALF BILLION YEARS AGO, our cosmic neighborhood was in chaos. In this age of formation and change, it was not yet recognizable as the solar system we know today. Some time after our sun appeared and burst into light, the clouds of gas and dust surrounding it swirled and collided, creating a flattened disk. Inside this turbulent pancake of particles and gases, tiny grains of dust fused into larger pieces. Collecting more and more grains as they swirled, these pieces eventually grew into gigantic spheres of molten rock and gases. These spheres, called protoplanets, eventually became the planets we recognize today.

During this same period, stray objects moved wildly around the early solar system. With so many objects flying around, it wasn't a surprise that they sometimes collided. About 20 to 100 million years after the formation of Earth, our young planet experienced a cosmic collision with an object the size of Mars. The result? The birth of our moon. For millions of years, protoplanets, asteroids, comets, and moons continued to smash and crash into each other. This messy and violent time also saw the gas and ice giant planets like Jupiter, Saturn, Uranus, and Neptune shift back and forth in their orbits before finally settling down to where we find them today. As they moved, they deflected large amounts of rocky debris toward the sun. This rubble—some more than six miles (9.5 km) in diameter—pounded the smaller rocky worlds.

On Earth, little evidence of this formative time period remains. Winds, rain, erosion, floods, volcanic eruptions, and the movement of crustal plates have erased most of these ancient impact sites. Yet on Mercury, Mars, and our moon, many of these early scars remain. What's more, the impacts may have caused rocks to blast off the surfaces of these inner worlds, sending them flying. On Earth, geologists have recovered rocks from the moon, Mars, and possibly even Mercury and Venus. Our Earth is a museum of rock samples from other worlds.

With so many **OBJECTS** flying around, it wasn't a surprise that they sometimes **COLLIDED.**

Small and large impacts were common during this fierce period, but no other impacts, except maybe one with Mars, resulted in the formation of a moon. This primitive smashup also changed Earth's rotational angle (or tilt of the planet) to 23.5 degrees from its axis. This tilt established future seasonal changes here on Earth, just as we know them today.

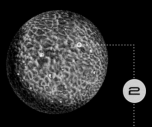

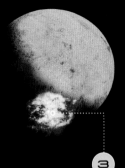

1

After a major smashup involving Earth and a Mars-size object, the moon condensed out of earthly dust rings roughly 4.5 billion years ago.

2

As the moon cooled, the surface solidified into a solid crust. More violent changes were about to take place.

3

THE EVOLUTION
OF THE MOON

◉ IN ITS INFANCY, our new moon was just a collection of bits of rock. Captured by Earth's newly expanded gravitational field, the debris spread out into a delicate ring structure. It would have looked a lot like Saturn's rings.

For the next few million years, the debris orbiting Earth continued to collide and weld together, steadily growing to form our moon. When the moon's spin on its axis slowed down to equal the speed it orbits around Earth, the moon cooled into an oblong, or lemon shape, with the two pointy ends directed toward and away from Earth. From Earth, the angle we see the moon at is deceiving. To us it appears perfectly round, like a big cosmic ball.

The next few billion years brought more impacts, followed by volcanic activity that gushed dark molten lava onto the side of the moon facing Earth. Finally, the moon's surface cooled and became the way it looks today.

Roughly 4.3 billion years ago, a gargantuan-size asteroid about 125 miles (200 km) in diameter slammed into the far side of the moon, creating the South Pole–Aitken Basin. Some 1,600 miles (2,500 km) in diameter and 8 miles (13 km) deep, it forms one of the largest known impact craters in the solar system.

Earth is a planet, and the moon is a satellite that orbits Earth. About one-quarter the size of Earth, our moon has no oxygen atmosphere or flowing water on its surface to support life.

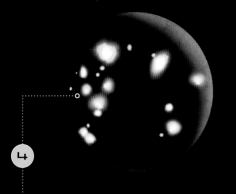

4 About 4.1 to 3.8 billion years ago, something, perhaps the movements of the outer planets, caused rocky debris to fly in toward the sun. This rubble pounded the surface of the moon.

5 About one billion years ago, the last of the large asteroid impacts ended. The moon's near side—the side facing Earth—broke out into volcanic activity, sending vast oceans of molten lava out over the lowland areas.

7 Today, the moon's surface is a record of its formation. The lava beds were mistaken by early observers as seas because they look blue in the daytime sky here on Earth. They named them *maria*—the Latin name for "lunar seas." Many people claim to see different images in these dark patches. Some envision the Woman in the Moon carrying a bundle on her back, or the face of the Man in the Moon. Others say they see two frog sisters or even a rabbit! Gaze at the moon next time when it is full. What do you see?

6 Less than a billion years ago, many of the smaller and intermediate-size craters that we see today were formed by impacts with the moon's surface. The younger craters have starlike ray patterns radiating out from their centers. These ray patterns were created when an impact caused light-colored rock lying under the moon's surface to blast out and then gently settle back down onto the surface.

EARTH AND MOON:
COMPARED

ALTHOUGH EARTH AND THE MOON WERE FORGED OUT OF SIMILAR MATERIALS, below the surface, their interiors are different. Both have molten cores made of pure iron; the center being solid and the outer parts soft and pliable.

The mantles of Earth and the moon are both made of rock. But here's where our makeups start to differ. Earth's upper mantle of hot fluid rock combined with its lower mantle of solid rock make up the thickest layer of our planet. In comparison, the moon's lithosphere—the solid part of the moon—is rock measuring approximately 620 miles (1,000 km) thick. It makes up most of the moon's interior.

The moon's surface, or crust, is made of just one type of rock—basalt. The dark gray rock forms a layer 37 to 93 miles (60–150 km) thick called regolith. Although it is made of loose deposits of dust, soil, and broken rubble, it is so hard it resembles concrete. The Apollo astronauts needed a hammer to pound core-sampling units into it. Earth's crust, on the other hand, is made of different materials. Earth's ocean floors are made of basaltic rock up to 5 miles (8 km) thick. The lighter continental crust is made of granite 40 miles (65 km) thick, which sits on top of basalt.

It's not just the makeups of our two worlds that differ, it's also how the bodies themselves behave. On Earth, volcanic activity continually occurs where the ocean floor slides underneath the edges of the continental plates. On the moon, there's no evidence that plates of crust ever formed. Instead, the volcanic activity that formed the maria resulted from a large patch of radioactive uranium that acted like a giant oven broiler. It melted the mantle rock, causing it to bubble up to the surface and flow out over the lowlands. Since that time, volcanic activity on the moon has mostly stopped. (Although deep underground, the near side of the moon remains a few hundred degrees hotter than the far side.) The hot molten rock inside the moon has become so dense it is now too heavy to rise up to the surface and flow out over the lunar landscape.

> The **VOLCANIC ACTIVITY** that formed the maria resulted from a large patch of radioactive uranium.

The interior of both Earth and the moon remain hot and molten. Unlike the moon, magma from Earth's mantle, powered by active volcanoes, still erupts onto the surface.

Crust

Upper Mantle

Lower Mantle

Outer Core

Inner Core

LUNAR FACT SHEET

Mean Distance from Earth:
239,000 miles (384,600 km)

Length of Lunar Day:
27.3 Earth days

Diameter:
2,160 miles (3,476 km)

Surface Temperature (day):
273°F (134°C)

Surface Temperature (night):
-245°F (-154°C)

Gravity:
⅙ Earth's

EARTH FACT SHEET

Length of Day:
24 hours

Diameter:
7,917 miles (12,741 km)

Highest Temperature:
136°F (58°C)

Lowest Temperature:
-126°F (-88°C)

Inner Core

Outer Core

Rock Mantle

Crust

TAKE ME TO THE
DARK SIDE

EARTH TAKES ABOUT 24 HOURS (ONE DAY) to complete one rotation on its axis. The moon takes 27 days to complete one rotation. This is about the same amount of time it takes the moon to complete one orbit around our planet. As a result of this close synchronization, one side of the moon always faces toward Earth, while the far side remains hidden from view. This synchronization is called tidal locking. Interestingly, tidal locking has been observed in most of the other major moons in our solar system.

The "dark side" of the moon may sound mysterious, but this side does actually experience just as much daylight shining down on it as the near side facing Earth. We just don't see it. Yet, the far side does hold surprises. When the Soviet Luna 3 spacecraft orbited the moon in 1959, it sent back the first images of this unseen surface. Astronomers were stunned to see that, unlike the side we can observe from Earth, there are no dark maria (plains) on this side. Instead, they saw a mess of craters strewn everywhere—craters piled on top of other craters, creating a rough, chaotic terrain.

We still don't know why the two faces of the moon look so different. One surprising idea is called the two-moon theory. When Earth collided with the Mars-size object, two moons may actually have grown out of the rings, one large and one small. The smaller of the two moons may have contained more radioactive material than the larger. Eventually, if the moons merged, it would have been this hot radioactive material that powered the volcanic activity on the near side, leaving the far side filled with craters.

With the moon's rotation and revolution periods both taking roughly 27 days to complete, only one side of the moon always faces Earth. We never see the far side!

As the Russian Luna 3 spacecraft orbited the moon in 1959, a great surprise was in store. It discovered that the far side of the moon (above) looks very different from the near side (right). There are no flat dark plains on the far side. It is covered in impact craters.

OTHER MOONS

TODAY, THERE ARE AT LEAST 181 KNOWN MOONS ORBITING THE PLANETS IN OUR SOLAR SYSTEM. Mercury and Venus, the two closest planets to the sun, have no satellites. Mars has two tiny potato-shaped moons resembling asteroids or big space rocks. Jupiter has 79 moons, making it the Grand Moon Champion! Four of these moons are easily visible through binoculars. Jupiter's Ganymede is bigger than the planet Mercury. The moon Io, with its surface splashed in orange, yellow, and red sulfur deposits, is the most active volcanic world in the solar system. Two of Jupiter's moons, Europa and Ganymede—and possibly its third moon—may have vast oceans hidden beneath icy outer shells.

Saturn has 53 known satellites and another nine that have likely been spotted. Saturn's largest moon is Titan. This spooky-looking moon is blanketed in a thick pumpkin-colored atmosphere, rich in nitrogen and methane gas. Scattered across its frozen surface are vast lakes of liquid methane that are dotted with floating icebergs. This landscape may be the perfect hiding place for life beyond Earth.

Icy planet Uranus has 27 moons, including tiny Miranda, which boasts the tallest cliffs in the solar system. Measuring three to six miles (5 to 10 km) high, some are 10 times higher than the walls of Earth's majestic Grand Canyon!

Farther from the sun, Neptune has 14 moons, including Triton, which many scientists believe is a dwarf planet that was captured by the planet's gravitational force. The dwarf planet Pluto has five moons of its own.

When comparing sizes of moons with their planets, our moon, being one-quarter the diameter of Earth, is considered to be supersize. Jupiter's moons may be bigger than our moon, but when compared with the diameter of Jupiter, their size ratio is much smaller. The only other body to have an abnormally large-size moon is Pluto. Its moon Charon measures about half the diameter of Pluto. For this reason, many astronomers classify Pluto and Charon as a double dwarf planet—the only one of its kind in our solar system. Yay, Pluto!

> When comparing sizes of moons with their planets, our moon is considered to be SUPERSIZE.

Ganymede

Titan

Callisto

Earth

Triton

Europa

Moon

Io

Charon/Pluto

Miranda

Phobos/Deimos

Moons in our solar system come in a variety of shapes and sizes. Some, like Titan, have atmospheres, and others, like Io, have active volcanoes. Moons Europa, Ganymede, and possibly Callisto also appear to have deep oceans of liquid water hidden beneath icy surfaces.

MOON MYTHS

MYTHS ARE ANCIENT TRADITIONAL TALES OR STORIES that attempted to explain natural or social phenomena. They were told generation to generation, changing over time depending on who the storyteller was.

For ancient Greeks, when lightning struck and thunder roared across the landscape, that was the god Zeus throwing lightning bolts to the ground. In ancient China, when the sun disappeared from view during a solar eclipse, it was because a dragon was eating it. People would bang drums and shoot off fireworks to scare it away!

A common European folktale tells the fate of a husband and wife caught working on a holy day. Their punishment was separation for the rest of their lives. They were each presented with a choice: freeze on the moon or sizzle on the sun. The wife chose the sun—she liked warm weather. The husband was left with the moon, where you can still see him today. That's right! He's the mythical Man in the Moon.

During a new moon, Romans believed it was a good time to cut your hair and fingernails to promote quick and healthy regrowth. It was also a good time to have teeth pulled. It was common knowledge in medieval Europe that the new moon was a good time to plant potatoes, pick apples, catch fish, place fence

When the sun mysteriously began disappearing from view, that was **A DRAGON** eating it.

Many ancient peoples believed that supernatural activities caused natural events. The Greeks thought when lightning and thunder struck, it must be the god Zeus throwing lightning bolts across the skies.

Different cultures, including ancient Chinese and Armenian, believed solar eclipses were caused by dragons eating the sun.

• • • • •

posts, and gather fresh dew. Under the beams of the full moon was the best time to harvest grapes, pick mushrooms, trap crabs, plant berries, and catch moonbeams in a box to save them for later.

It seemed to many people of the past that moonlight and moonbeams were special. They held some sort of magical powers. People practicing ancient folk remedies believed the moon cured sickness and influenced health and recovery. For centuries, epilepsy was considered to be a lunar affliction.

In parts of England, the folk cure for whooping cough was to have the afflicted child lay on the cold ground under moonlight and expose their stomach to healing moonbeams. No doubt these remedies may seem "loony" to us today, but before modern medicine, people sought answers from nature.

Today, we know the moon isn't actually responsible for any magical cures or powers. And we also know that the moon doesn't radiate any light of its own. It, like all members of our solar system, shines brightly because of sunlight reflecting off its surface. Beautiful moonlight, then, is actually just secondhand sunlight!

THERE IS SOMETHING ODD ABOUT THIS PHOTO. Can you figure out what it is? The answer is on page 63.

HOWL IF YOU'VE HEARD THIS ONE

MOON MYTHS AND LUNAR LANGUAGE

"THERE MUST BE A FULL MOON OUT TONIGHT." Have you ever said that when something goes wrong? Full moons and moonlight have sometimes been feared. The idea that full moons are linked to bad or weird things happening goes back a long, long time.

Classical Greek philosopher Aristotle and Roman historian Pliny the Elder both observed that the human brain contains a considerable amount of water. In fact, the human body is almost 60 percent water. That's so much water, they figured, the moon must pull on our bodies the same way it pulls on Earth's oceans. All that tugging by the moon might influence the human body in peculiar ways.

Throughout Europe during the Middle Ages, people were certain full moons transformed some humans into werewolves. The Old English word *wer* means "man." Werewolves, or manwolves, were thought to be shape-shifting creatures with uncontrollable rage and huge appetites. They attacked livestock and, occasionally, an unlucky human out after dark. If you were bitten but escaped an attack, under every full moon that followed, you would shape-shift into a werewolf, too! You'd spend the night running through the countryside, howling at the moon. Werewolves were the most common shape-shifters in the night, but there were also were-foxes, were-bears, were-snakes, and even were-rabbits! Run away! Run away!

Even in the 21st century, some believers still think the mystical power of the full moon causes erratic behavior in people. Some believers still think crime rates suddenly rise and more robberies take place. Others are certain emergency room visits go up, births increase, more traffic accidents occur, and even dog bites increase! In fact, we still use the Roman goddess of the moon's name to describe someone acting a little strangely. Her name was Luna, the basis for the word "lunatic."

Luckily, scientific studies have not turned up any evidence to support the idea that a full moon has any physical influence on human beings. Except, maybe, that its bright light might cause some people unrestful sleep, making them cranky the next day.

> The idea that full moons are linked to bad or WEIRD THINGS happening goes back a long, long time.

Throughout Europe during the Middle Ages, people were certain **FULL MOONS** transformed some humans into **WERE- WOLVES.**

In this illustration a werewolf prowls the English countryside late at night, sniffing the air searching for prey. It might be a sheep not bedded down for the night or an unlucky farmer walking home from town.

WHAT'S IN A NAME?

AS THE FULL MOON PHASE APPROACHES, you can't help but notice its increasing presence in the sky. Of all the phases of the moon, the full moon is the most celebrated and most feared. You may even have heard some special names for different full moons. Some date back hundreds of years. Many descriptive names were used to keep track of the seasons or the way in which humans and animals responded to weather.

So, what's with all the weird moon names we hear today? There are supermoons, a term invented to describe when the moon appears a tiny percentage larger than it did the month before; full wolf moons, when hungry wolves howl at night; full strawberry moons, a time for harvesting strawberries; full worm moons, when the ground defrosts and earthworms start crawling out from their burrows; full sap moons, when maple trees are tapped to make maple syrup; full pink moons, when fruit blossoms come out; and full fish moons, when shad swim upstream to spawn.

All in all, there are more than a hundred different names for a full moon. The two most famous full moons are blue moons and harvest moons. Have you heard the phrase "once in a blue moon"? Blue moons aren't really colored blue. They occur when a month has two full moons in it. It's a fairly rare occurrence. Harvest moons occur in late September or early October, when the extra light cast down on the fields

All in all, there are more than **100 DIFFERENT** names for a full moon.

Harvest moons occur in late September or early October. Rising majestically at sunset, the bright moonlight aids farmers by giving them more time to harvest their summer crops before colder winter temperatures set in.

allows farmers to work late into the evening harvesting crops.

Many cultures around the world tie festivals to either full moons or new moons. Chinese New Year begins at the first new moon between January 21 and February 16. That's when day and night are equal in length. In Japan, the equinoxes are a time to honor ancestors. Persians also celebrate the vernal equinox as a new year with the festival of Nowruz. The first full moon after the vernal equinox is when Passover occurs, a time of celebration for those of the Jewish faith. And for those of the Christian faith, the first Sunday after the first full moon following the vernal equinox brings Easter.

During the Chinese Moon Festival, which occurs during the closest full moon to the autumnal, or fall, equinox, people enjoy moon cakes, shoot off fireworks, and plant trees.

In this 1950s depiction, 24 hours after landing on the moon, equipment is unloaded and the cargo ships' fuel tanks are dismantled and placed on the lunar surface to be used as crew living quarters. The bright red star in the sky to the lower left of Earth is the planet Mars.

DREAMS OF EARLY EXPLORERS

A BELOVED VINTAGE SONG FROM THE 1950s requested that you "Fly Me to the Moon." For centuries, poets, writers, and dreamers contemplated voyages to the moon. But just how we would get there posed as many questions as what we might find if we did make it there.

Even as far back as the Middle Ages, fantastical engineering schemes and tales were considered around banquet tables. One such tale was published in a 1638 book written by Bishop Francis Godwin under the pen name Domingo Gonsales. The book was titled *The Man in the Moone*. In it, the hero stumbles upon a species of wild swans that can lift extremely heavy loads. Tethering them together with rope, after a few low-level flying adventures, he ends up on the moon. There he meets extremely tall Lunars, who live in a beautiful, perfect world.

In 1865, Jules Verne—the 19th-century author of *20,000 Leagues Under the Sea* and *From the Earth to the Moon*—suggested that the best way to get humankind to the moon was to shoot them out of a gigantic cannon. On their journey, Verne's three intrepid explorers experience weightlessness, jubilantly floating and bouncing off walls in their bullet-shaped space capsule, much like the first Apollo astronauts would do 104 years later!

In the 1950s, new technological advances helped sweep across the planet the idea that moon travel might actually be possible. During World War II, Germany had developed military missiles. Scientists now thought they could modify the power and shape of these rockets to carry humans into space. Experimenters, including German physicist Wernher von Braun, American astronomer Fred L. Whipple, engineer Willy Ley, and space artist Chesley Bonestell, began sketching out how this might be accomplished. They published their results in a book titled *Conquest of the Moon*, in which a 50-person lunar landing party arrives and explores the moon.

Finally, in 1969, the vision of these four pioneers—along with many other talented engineers and machinists—came true. American astronauts Neil Armstrong and Buzz Aldrin gently set down the lunar lander *Eagle* onto the moon's surface. As Armstrong declared to the world "the *Eagle* has landed," humans finally set foot on the moon.

Neil Armstrong declared to the world, "THE *EAGLE* HAS LANDED."

GREAT HOAXES
AND OTHER
REAL MYSTERIES

BIGFOOT, THE LOCH NESS MONSTER, and other strange tales have fascinated humanity across the ages. Are they true? Some people certainly think so, though most agree that they're nothing more than fun, fanciful stories. But what happens when a story intended to be fictional gets out of hand? That's just what happened in what became known as the Great Moon Hoax of 1835!

Likely written by journalist Richard Adams Locke, six stories were published in the daily newspaper the *New York Sun*. Though the stories were a spoof, a type of humorous fiction, readers believed every word! Locke's headlines announced that the famous astronomer Sir John Herschel, using a new powerful telescope in South Africa, had observed unicorns, two-legged beavers, and four-foot (1.2-m)-tall people with copper-colored hair and bat wings gently flying down cliffs and alighting on the ground—ON THE MOON! Even more intriguing, he said that Herschel had observed rushing rivers, a thick covering of green plants, and giant purple amethyst crystals.

On September 16, 1835, the *Sun* admitted the stories had been a hoax and published an apology. Some readers were angry, but most actually found the whole situation funny.

Transient lunar phenomena (TLPs) are the brightly colored lights or mists observed in lunar craters.

Though the Great Hoax was pure fantasy, there are some odd lunar occurrences that may, in fact, be real. Moon observers often claim to see changes on the lunar surface. Reports of transient lunar phenomena (TLPs) date back at least 1,000 years. On June 18, 1178, five monks living in Canterbury, England, watched as one of the horns of the waxing moon suddenly burst into flames and smoke. Did they witness a meteorite crashing into the moon? That's one explanation for it.

Since the telescope was invented in 1608, odd observations of the moon have ranged from foggy mists covering the floors of craters to changes in the surface's colors from gray to red, green, blue, or violet. Bright lights have been seen moving inside shadowed craters.

More than 2,000 events have been documented over time. Even the Apollo 11 astronauts were asked to investigate glowing lights seen near the crater Aristarchus as they orbited the moon.

What are these strange TLPs? They could be trapped gas escaping from underground cavities or flashes of light from meteorites impacting the surface. They could be electrostatic discharges, like the sparks that sometimes zap your finger when you reach out and touch a light switch.

Even amateur astronomers can spot TLPs. Using a telescope, carefully scan the Aristarchus plateau and the craters Plato, Grimaldi, Kepler, Copernicus, and Tycho. You might just see a flash of colorful lights.

Many people believed the Great Moon Hoax of 1835, which claimed that an astronomer had revealed that the moon was populated by wild creatures—including purple unicorns and humanlike bat-men with wings and copper-colored hair.

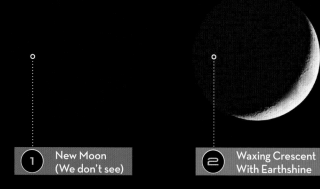

| 1 | New Moon (We don't see) |

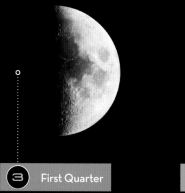

| 2 | Waxing Crescent With Earthshine |

| 3 | First Quarter |

| 4 | Waxing Gibbous |

THE CHANGING PHASES
OF THE MOON

THE SUN APPEARS CIRCULAR IN THE DAY-TIME SKY, but the moon's shape continuously changes, looking different from one evening to the next. These changes, however, always appear in a predictable pattern, known as the phases of the moon.

The moon does not change its physical shape throughout the month; what changes is the part of the moon illuminated by the sun that we're able to see. As the moon circles Earth—an orbit that takes 27.3 days—only one-half of the moon is fully illuminated at any time. As Earth travels on its own pathway around the sun, it moves slightly faster than the moon

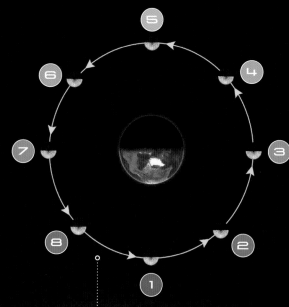

As the moon orbits Earth, only one side of the moon is illuminated by the sun. The amount of lunar surface we see is the result of the moon's position in relation to Earth and the sun.

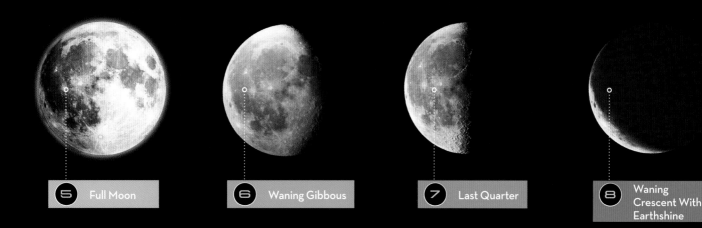

5 Full Moon	**6** Waning Gibbous	**7** Last Quarter	**8** Waning Crescent With Earthshine

through space. By the time the moon catches up to the same place in the sky it was one month earlier, 29.5 days have passed. This is known as one synodic month, and it is measured from one new moon to the next.

As the moon and Earth move through their orbits, the moon goes through eight designated phases. The shapes it takes are caused by its location in relation to the sun and where people are on Earth. The darkened new moon (#1)—when the moon is situated between Earth and the sun—is first. This phase is invisible to us on Earth. Following the new moon, a thin waxing crescent suddenly appears (#2). The word "waxing" is a term that describes something that is growing in size. Its opposite, "waning," means it is shrinking in size. The waxing moon, growing brighter during the month, finally reaches the full moon phase (#5). Then, it begins to wane and grow dimmer. Fourteen days pass from a new moon to a full moon phase, and about 14 days pass before the moon enters the next new moon phase again. One interesting thing the Apollo astronauts noticed was that Earth also goes through phases.

Looking out from the lunar surface, the changing phases of Earth were opposite those of the moon as seen by observers back home.

Depending on how clear the sky is, during the waxing and waning crescent phases, sharp eyes can detect a faint outline of the hidden full moon behind the brightly glowing crescent. The faint outline may even appear blue. We already know the bright crescent moon is being illuminated by the sun. But what is illuminating the dark side that should be cast in black shadow? This light is coming from Earth. You are seeing sunlight bouncing off our oceans and white cloud tops back onto the moon's dark surface of the moon. We call this phenomenon earthshine. What a curious and subtle reminder that our planet is also a shining globe floating in space.

This is an old Native American RIDDLE. Can you solve it?

What has two horns when young, loses them in middle age, and regains them in old age?

Answer: the moon

WHEN THE TIDE COMES IN

IN ADDITION TO ILLUMINATING THE NIGHT SKY, the moon also affects Earth in more dramatic ways. Combined with Earth's rotation, the gravitational pull of the moon and sun on Earth causes landmasses located near the Equator to bulge! Though you likely won't notice—the change is much too small to see. We're more familiar with the sun's and moon's effects on our oceans. Their combined gravitational forces cause the oceans' daily rise and fall. We refer to these time periods as high and low tides.

Typically, high and low tides occur twice in a 24-hour period. In open oceans, the average range of tidal change is about three feet (1 m) in height. Coastal tidal ranges can vary significantly depending on the shape of the shoreline, the ocean bottom, and the volume of water located directly offshore. For example, in the Mediterranean Sea, where coastal shorelines are very shallow, we won't find much difference in the height of tides. Thousands of miles away, the world's most dramatic and largest tidal range occurs in the Bay of Fundy in Canada. In just six hours, the water levels here can drop and rise a staggering

At low tides, hardy sea life is exposed to the air for a few hours. Clinging to the rocks, sea stars, anemones, and other sea creatures await the return of the higher tides.

When high tides return hours later, the shoreline waters rise and the natural underwater environment is restored.

The highest and lowest tides are known as spring tides. They occur when the sun, moon, and Earth are in a straight line.

Neap tides are not very high or low. They occur when the sun and moon form a 90-degree angle.

The moon AFFECTS EARTH in DRAMATIC WAYS.

50 feet (15 m) in height. How can the tides there vary so much? It has to do with the shape of the bay. First, the tide goes out, exposing the sandy ocean bottom. A few hours later, rising waters pushed together by the funnel-shaped bay charge back in. This results in the extreme changes in water height. Twice a day, the bay fills and empties—literally hundreds of billions of tons of water circulate during each cycle. This is more water than the flow in all of the world's freshwater rivers combined!

Predicting changes in tides is important for a variety of people, from sports enthusiasts to commercial fishers, whose livelihoods depend on the ocean. Large ships navigating through shallow ports or intercoastal waterways need to plan their schedules. Luckily, tides follow predictable patterns, and tide tables reliably provide this critical information. There are a few times of

year, though, when tides behave differently.

When the sun, moon, and Earth are all aligned, tides do something pretty neat. On one side of Earth, the moon's strong gravitational force pulls at the oceans, causing the water to surge outward, toward the moon. At the same time, on the opposite side of Earth, the sun tugs on Earth's water, causing it to surge toward the sun. When this happens, scientists call it a spring tide because the waters seem to spring away from Earth. You can see spring tides in action on the coast of California. Here, extreme high and low tidal changes can approach seven feet (2.1 m) during spring tides, compared to only about 2.5 feet (0.8 m) during the rest of the year.

Other times, when the sun, Earth, and moon are at right angles to each other, the gravitational forces are spread out, resulting in much smaller shifts in water levels. These are called neap tides.

LUNAR ECLIPSES

A TOTAL LUNAR ECLIPSE

MOON: During a total lunar eclipse, a full moon passes directly into Earth's shadow. Red sunlight filters through Earth's atmosphere and bounces off the moon, causing it to appear red.

SUN: As the sun shines brightly on the daytime side of Earth, some of its light passes around Earth and bounces off the moon, illuminating the eclipse side of the moon that faces Earth's nighttime side.

EARTH: During a total lunar eclipse, Earth aligns directly between the sun and moon, casting a shadow on the moon.

Volcanic eruptions on Earth can affect how we see total lunar eclipses!

A lunar eclipse from start to finish

THERE ARE THREE BASIC TYPES OF LUNAR ECLIPSES.

Penumbral lunar eclipses occur when the full moon passes through the faint outer edges of Earth's shadow. Partial lunar eclipses occur when part of the moon passes through Earth's darker central shadow. Total lunar eclipses, the most spectacular type, occur when the full moon passes directly through the center of Earth's shadow, resulting in a dramatic change to the moon's appearance. This rare event transforms the moon into a vibrant rust red orb in the sky.

With the moon making a full orbit around Earth every 27.3 days, you might expect to see a lunar eclipse occurring every time the moon is full. Yet, as you probably know from looking at the night sky, that's not the case. The reason lies in the tilt of the moon's orbit.

Picture the moon's and Earth's orbits as flat disks. The moon's orbit around Earth is tilted five degrees compared with Earth's orbit around the sun. This means the moon spends most of its time either above or below the flat disk of Earth's orbit. That keeps it out of Earth's shadow. Where there's no shadow, there's no eclipse! But two to four times a year, the moon does pass through part of Earth's shadow, and this is when a lunar eclipse can occur.

A total eclipse lasts about three and a half to four hours. It takes about an hour for the shadow of Earth to slowly creep across the face of the moon. Then, for almost an hour and a half, the moon turns an eerie reddish amber color as it passes through the heart of Earth's main shadow. Finally, the dark gray shadow recedes.

The moon's striking red color actually tells scientists a lot. During a total lunar eclipse, Earth blocks the sun's light, preventing most it from reaching the moon's surface. Some sunlight does pass through the edges of Earth's atmosphere, however. As sunlight passes through, the atmosphere filters out all the blue light waves. That means only red light waves reach the surface of the moon and bounce back to our eyes. But sometimes that expected red hue doesn't occur. When massive forest fires or erupting volcanoes on Earth have put a lot of smoke or debris into our atmosphere, the moon almost disappears from view. Pollution in our skies does not permit red wavelengths of light to pass through and illuminate the lunar surface. In this way, a lunar eclipse tells scientists a great deal about the conditions of the air we breathe.

This RARE EVENT transforms the moon into a vibrant rust red orb in the sky.

SOLAR ECLIPSES

SOLAR ECLIPSES, LIKE LUNAR ECLIPSES, occur as a result of the alignment of Earth, the sun, and the moon. Yet solar eclipses are so rare that you would be lucky to see one in your lifetime.

These events only occur when a new moon passes between Earth and the sun. In a total solar eclipse, the moon, sun, and Earth are exactly lined up. When that happens, the moon completely blocks our view of the sun. The sky turns dark, and the sun is hidden from sight.

Sometimes during a solar eclipse, a bright glowing ring of sunlight shines around the moon. This kind of solar eclipse is called an annular eclipse. It occurs when the sun and moon are in alignment with Earth but the moon is at its farthest point from Earth—the moon visually appears smaller than the sun and does not completely block its light.

In a partial solar eclipse, only a portion of the sun is blocked. This kind of eclipse takes place when the sun and moon are almost—but

A TOTAL SOLAR ECLIPSE

SUN: A total solar eclipse occurs on the daytime side of Earth when the moon passes directly between Earth and the sun.

MOON: When a new moon passes across the day-time sky, it causes a shadow to fall on Earth. Follow the lines in this diagram from the sun to see how sunlight passes around the moon, forming a triangle of shadow to fall on Earth.

EARTH: Only a small portion of Earth is in the moon's full shadow during a solar eclipse. This portion experiences a total solar eclipse. Areas nearby experience a partial solar eclipse.

not exactly—aligned. When this happens, the moon obscures only a portion of the sun, making it look like a bite has been chomped out of it.

Eclipses are reoccurring natural phenomena here on Earth. Yet there are only a few other spots in our solar system that also experience total solar eclipses. Mercury and Venus don't have any moons, so solar eclipses can't occur there. The moons of Mars, Jupiter, and Saturn are too small to block out the sun, so they're off the list, too. Hanging out in the rings of Saturn, you might experience the passage of one of its many moons across the face of the sun, but daytime certainly would not be turned into night.

Even here on Earth it's not a guarantee that you'll see a total solar eclipse. The path of totality—the area on Earth's surface where the total solar eclipse has the right conditions for viewing—may be up to 166 miles (267 km) wide. View the sky from anywhere outside this pathway, and you might see only a partial eclipse or miss it completely!

With such a small percentage of Earth covered by a total solar eclipse, people travel the world to witness this stunning cosmic event. Using special solar glasses to block out the bright sunlight, viewers watch and wait as a small dark sliver on the sun steadily grows larger as the moon moves into position.

Suddenly, the sky goes dark and the sun disappears. Stars come out. Familiar constellations pop into view. Warm winds brush across your cheeks, and confused birds begin roosting in trees as if night has fallen. A shimmering halo of light surrounds the darkened solar disk, forming a magnificent crown. This jagged ring of light is called the solar corona. It is the outer atmosphere of the sun, which is normally hidden in the bright daytime sky.

Then, just as quickly, the brilliant sun begins to reappear, turning night back into day as the moon continues along its never-ending path around Earth. This awe-inspiring experience is over—until the next time the grand event occurs.

LIFE WITHOUT A MOON

WITHOUT OUR MOON, life on Earth might be very different. Days would be much shorter and seasons would never change or be wild and erratic. It would be pitch-black every night of the year. There would be no eclipses of the sun or the moon to wow us, no rising harvest moons to inspire songs and stories, no supermoons, blue moons, or worm moons. Earth might wobble on its axis like a dangerously spinning top, creating 100-mile-an-hour (160-km/h) winds, spawning massive hurricanes.

Most important, life as we know it might not exist. That's right: Without a moon, Earth might not have the complex, diverse life that surrounds us today.

Without the moon,
LIFE AS WE KNOW IT
might not exist.

Earth is 4.5 billion years old. Fossil evidence shows that the first, simplest life-forms appeared 700 million years after it formed. Less than a half billion years ago, all life on Earth was still living in the seas.

If you were to travel back in time 420 million years, put on a diving mask, and look below the surface of the Silurian Sea, you would be shocked by what greeted you. The oceans were swarming with bizarre and colorful creatures scurrying around the sandy bottom or swimming freely through crystal blue waters. If you were to surface and look around, you'd see mounds of hardened black lava poking above the foaming waves. There would be no palm trees—or any trees for that matter. They didn't exist yet. Only a few species of hardy green plants would have transitioned onto land.

So how is the moon responsible for the transition to life on land? You know that the gravitational pull of the moon creates high and low tides. You may also be familiar with tide pools, which become exposed to air once the tide recedes. That was the case millions of years ago, too. Over time, the resilient life-forms that populated tide pools evolved new adaptations that allowed them to better survive during dry spells. Eventually, they were able to leave the oceans behind and live on land. It was these early land explorers that evolved into amphibians, dinosaurs, birds, insects, snakes, and mammals like you and me. Without the moon, Earth might be a profoundly different world, populated with very basic life still mostly living in the oceans.

Somewhere between 530 million and 430 million years ago, centipede-like creatures began emerging from the seas to explore exposed volcanic lava rocks above water. Plants colonizing these bare rocks soon created a landscape rich in food resources and paved the way for later, more advanced forms of life.

NEW LANDS
FOR YOU TO EXPLORE

IMAGINE BEING ABLE TO EXPLORE AN EXOTIC LAND 239,000 MILES (384,600 km) away without traveling anywhere. All you need is a small telescope and this map to guide you along your journey.

The moon is a prime target for many new space observers because it's easy to find and its wealth of details are visible using even the smallest of instruments. Sweeping your telescope across the lunar surface, mountain ranges, vast lava plains, and magnificent craters come into view. Explore the terminator for the most rewarding views. The terminator is the line that divides the nighttime side from the

Explore the **TERMINATOR** for the most rewarding views.

daytime side on the moon. Along this line you can observe high-contrast details inside craters and mountain ranges. Sharp eyes can sometimes even pick out the sunlit tops of mountain peaks.

For best viewing, wait until the moon is high in the sky. Earth's atmosphere is thinner in this area of the sky, so it will interfere less with your moon views. The moon's phases can also help you pick the best time for viewing. It's easiest to explore the moon during the first 14 days of its cycle (the days leading up to the full moon). After that, the moon rises 40 to 50 minutes later each evening, at points not appearing above the horizon until after 1 a.m. (Maybe don't do this on a school night!)

Begin your observations using your telescope's lowest power, so that the entire moon is visible. The maria, large craters, and brightly lit mountain peaks should all pop into view. Upping your telescope's power to 100x magnification, you can now explore individual craters, as well as rough mountainous terrain. At 200x magnification, you're a real lunar explorer! The view through your eyepiece is what the Apollo astronauts would have seen just before they began orbiting the moon.

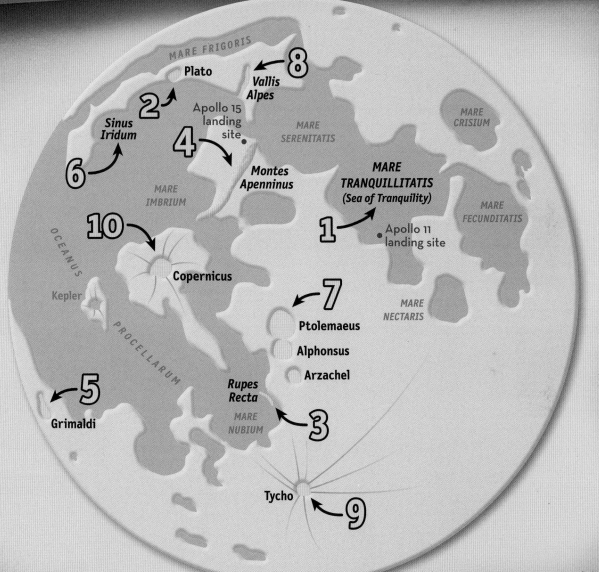

MARE FRIGORIS

Plato

2

8 Vallis Alpes

MARE SERENITATIS

Sinus Iridum

6

Apollo 15 landing site

4

Montes Apenninus

MARE TRANQUILLITATIS (Sea of Tranquility)

1

Apollo 11 landing site

MARE CRISIUM

MARE FECUNDITATIS

MARE IMBRIUM

O C E A N U S

Kepler

10

Copernicus

7

Ptolemaeus

Alphonsus

Arzachel

MARE NECTARIS

P R O C E L L A R U M

Rupes Recta

MARE NUBIUM

3

5

Grimaldi

Tycho

9

Here are the top 10 coolest sites that can be seen on the moon using a small telescope.

LUNAR FEATURES

WE MAY NOT BE ABLE TO GO TO THE MOON TODAY, but we can still take a lunar field trip. To start, here are some types of geological features found on the moon. Learn about them, and then we'll head out to see some of the most famous lunar sights.

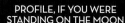

PHOTO, AS SEEN FROM ABOVE	PROFILE, IF YOU WERE STANDING ON THE MOON

MARIA

When viewing these large, flat expanses, early astronomers thought they were seeing water on the moon. So they named these areas *maria* (pronounced MAR-ee-a), which is Latin for "seas." Today, we know each *mare* (pronounced MAR-ay) is a large, flat volcanic plain, and that together, all the maria cover about one-fifth of the lunar surface facing Earth.

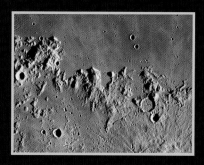

MOUNTAINS

On Earth, mountains are created by lava flowing out of volcanoes or large plates of rock crashing into each other. On the moon, mountains form when asteroids or large meteorites smash into the ground. These impacts toss out debris, creating mountain ranges, or *montes*. The tallest mountain, or *mons*, on the moon is Mons Huygens. It is 3.4 miles (5.5 km) high. By comparison, Mount Everest on Earth is 5.5 miles (8.85 km) high.

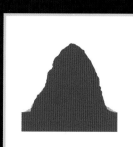

RILLES

Rille (pronounced ril) is a German word that means "groove." On the moon, rilles are long, narrow valleys that look like dried-up riverbeds. But instead of water, it was flowing lava that cut these snakelike channels.

》》》》 RAYS

Rays are the result of light-colored dust and rock being blasted out of craters and then gently settling back down onto the lunar surface. They resemble the thin spokes of a wheel radiating out from the hub. Craters with rays are young craters, sometimes no more than a few hundred million years old.

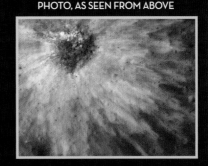

》》》》 CRATERS

Craters are cup-shaped holes in the ground that are formed by impacts from asteroids or other space debris. They range in size from microscopic to 180 miles (290 km) in diameter. The smallest craters you can see with an amateur telescope are about 2 to 3 miles (3.2–4.8 km) in diameter. Large craters are labeled as walled plains or ringed plains.

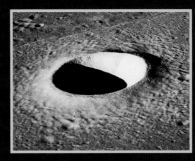
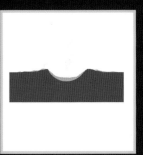

》》》》 WALLED PLAINS

Walled plains are large, smooth-floored craters surrounded by low, circular walls with no central peak sticking up in the center. They can range in size from 37 to 180 miles (60–290 km) in diameter.

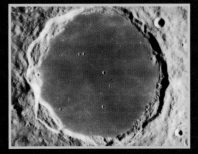
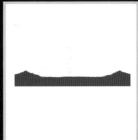

》》》》 RINGED PLAINS

Ringed plains are deeper craters that have floors sometimes jumbled with debris. A ringed plain may also have a sharp-pointed peak poking up from the center, caused by the ground rebounding during the impact that caused the crater. Steep walls shaped like steps surround these craters' edges.

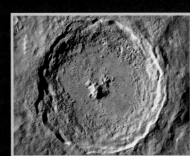

Apollo 11 landing site

>>>>> SEA OF TRANQUILITY

The Sea of Tranquility (Mare Tranquillitatis) is a large mare that was created about 4.5 billion years ago. It was the landing site for the Apollo 11 mission and the home of the first human footprints on the lunar surface. The Sea of Tranquility is roughly 540 miles (870 km) in diameter. To the Apollo astronauts, it appeared to be one gigantic flat plain strewn with boulders that had been ejected during the formation of distant craters. The glare of sunlight hampered the astronauts' vision, though the landscape jumped out at them with unbelievable clarity without air to obscure the view. The whole world seemed to curve around them, making the distant horizon feel unnaturally close (a side effect of the moon being only one-quarter the size of Earth).

>>>>> PLATO

The walled plain Plato was named after the famous Greek philosopher who lived more than 2,300 years ago. Nicknamed the Great Black Lake, it is one of the darkest spots on the moon and was formed after the Late Heavy Bombardment 3.8 billion years ago. Through a telescope, it looks like an oval crater set into rocky terrain. But its oval shape is deceptive. When viewed straight-on from lunar orbit, it is actually quite round, spanning about 68 miles (110 km) in diameter and with walls reaching up 1.2 miles (2 km) above the floor. When the terminator line is near this crater, you can watch the shape of the shadows change in just a matter of minutes.

Looking out over the Sea of Tranquility, future explorers may be more fortunate than the heroic Apollo astronauts were, as they may have a chance to witness a total eclipse of the sun from the moon! As Earth passes between the moon and the sun, the moon's surface is cast in an eerie red glow. Brilliant stars shine above—an unusual sight on the moon!—and the outer corona, or outer atmosphere of the sun, shines brilliantly around Earth's dark surface.

The towering Straight Wall (Rupes Recta) is the giant vertical cliff stretching almost 70 miles (110 km) across the face of the moon. At nearly 1,000 feet (300 m) high, it's taller than a 100-story building. But because the moon exerts only one-sixth Earth's gravity, you might try to free-climb the Straight Wall. In a space suit, that would represent quite a feat!

RUPES RECTA

Rupes Recta is a Latin name that means "straight cliff." The popular name used by astronomers for Rupes Recta is the Straight Wall. Through a telescope, it certainly looks like a long, straight wall, but here's the interesting part: It isn't a wall and it isn't straight! It is a linear fault that runs 68 miles (110 km) in length, with a height of about 787 to 995 feet (240–300 m). A fault appears when part of the ground suddenly rises up or drops down. The Straight Wall formed when a long crack in the lava floor split and the ground buckled and pushed up. That formed a long, tall cliff.

MONTES APENNINUS

If any feature on the moon could take a prize for being the most striking to view through a telescope, the rugged mountain range Montes Apenninus would be it. Named after the Apennine Mountains in Italy, this lunar chain formed when the nearby Imbrium Basin was blasted into creation by an impact four billion years ago. Mountain ranges on Earth take millions of years to grow. The Montes Apenninus range was created in just minutes, as the shock wave from the nearby impact rippled the lunar surface. Stretching over 370 miles (600 km) in length, the range includes more than 3,000 peaks. The Apollo 15 mission made its historic landing between two of the larger peaks, Mons Hadley and Mons Hadley Delta, on July 26, 1971.

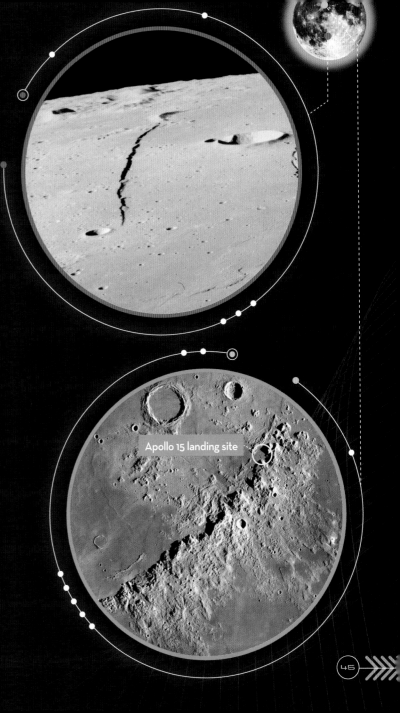

Apollo 15 landing site

GRIMALDI

The crater Grimaldi may be one of the strangest areas to explore on the moon. The dark shade of the floor contrasts with the brighter surrounding walls, making it an easy target to observe. This walled plain covers an area of about 15,000 square miles (38,000 sq km), making it larger than the U.S. states of Vermont, Delaware, and Rhode Island combined. Here astronomers have glimpsed strange flashes of light or orange-and-green-tinted vapor glowing dimly, and occasional fuzzy patches of fog may materialize above this ancient lava floor. Sensitive instruments aboard orbiting lunar spacecraft have also spotted areas where carbon dioxide gas is leaking out from inside the moon, which may be the cause of these strange occurrences.

SINUS IRIDUM

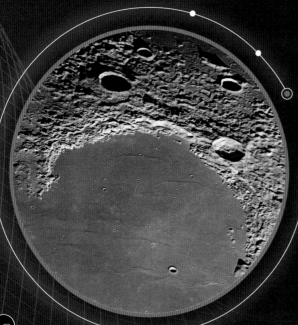

Sinus Iridum is a Latin name meaning "bay of rainbows." You might think this is a pretty odd name for a place on a dry, airless world where there are no clouds and it never rains. The name for this wide, flat plain came from its half-circular shape. Bordered by the Montes Jura, it looks like an arching rainbow! The Sinus Iridum is the remains of a gigantic impact crater that flooded with lava 3.7 to 3.2 billion years ago. Apollo 1 rock samples tell us the surface we see through a telescope formed 3.3 billion years ago. The walls surrounding the bay tower 9,850 feet (3,000 m) above the bay floor. Sinus Iridum is located on the edge of the Mare Imbrium, or the Sea of Rains, which formed 3.8 billion years ago during a collision with a giant asteroid.

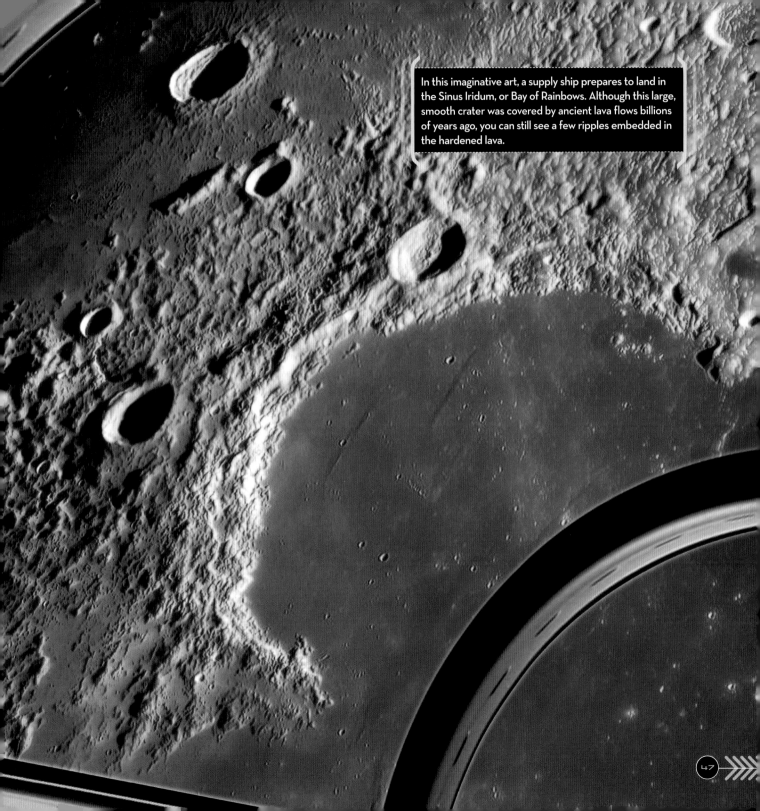

In this imaginative art, a supply ship prepares to land in the Sinus Iridum, or Bay of Rainbows. Although this large, smooth crater was covered by ancient lava flows billions of years ago, you can still see a few ripples embedded in the hardened lava.

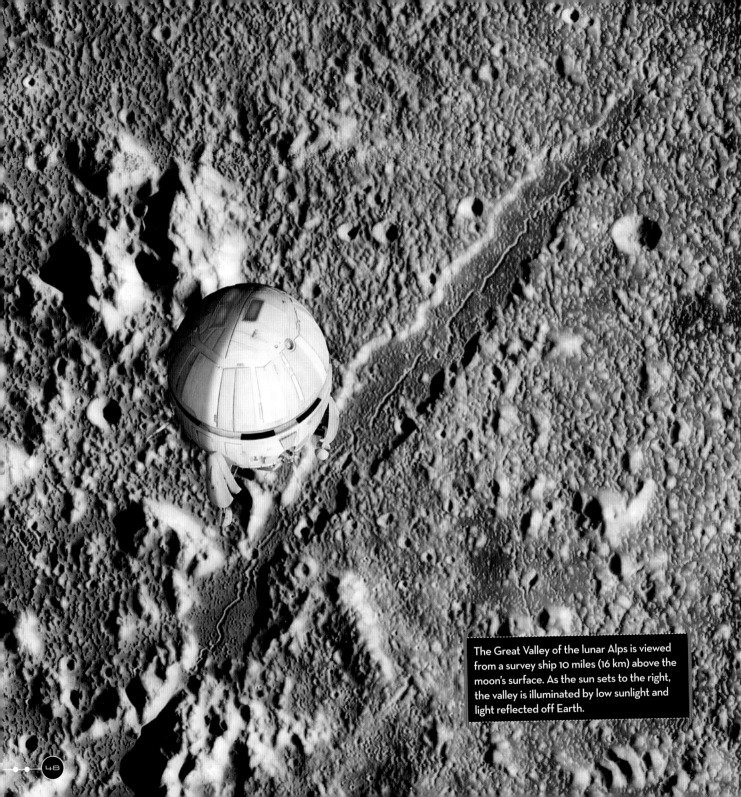

The Great Valley of the lunar Alps is viewed from a survey ship 10 miles (16 km) above the moon's surface. As the sun sets to the right, the valley is illuminated by low sunlight and light reflected off Earth.

PTOLEMAEUS, ALPHONSUS, AND ARZACHEL

These craters, called the Three Amigos, form an easy-to-spot chain. Ptolemaeus was named after Ptolemy, the second-century Roman astronomer-mathematician of Egyptian descent. Measuring 95 miles (153 km) wide, it is the largest and oldest of the three craters. The smooth floor was flooded with lava billions of years ago.

The middle crater, Alphonsus, was named after the Spanish king Alfonso X of Castile. It measures 74 miles (119 km) wide, and its floor is fractured with rilles. Its central peak rises almost a mile (1.6 km) above the crater bottom. Careful observers can sometimes spot six dark patches inside this crater, too. These are thought to be the result of volcanic explosions that showered the surface with tiny dark glass beads.

The smallest crater, Arzachel, is a relatively young impact crater. It's named after the famous Arab astronomer and mathematician Abu Ishaq Ibrahim al-Zarqali. Measuring 60 miles (96 km) wide, it has staircase-shaped terraces along the crater rim.

VALLIS ALPES

Vallis Alpes is a Latin name meaning "alpine valley." Stretching 80 miles (129 km) long and 6 miles (10 km) wide, this valley cuts right through the center of the Montes Alpes, or lunar Alps. Geologists call this type of feature a *graben*—a German word for "ditch" or "trench." Grabens form between two fault lines, or moving plates where land suddenly drops down.

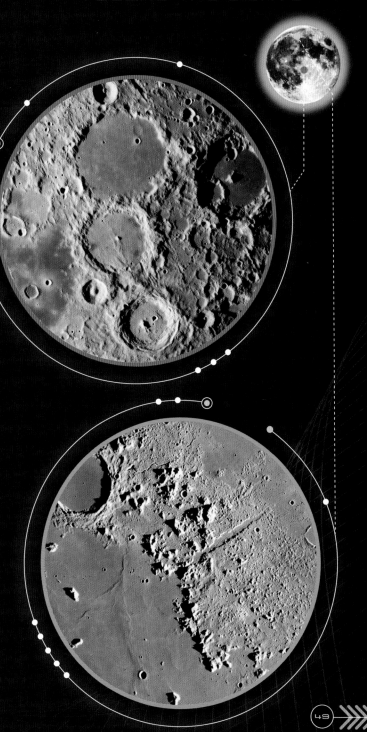

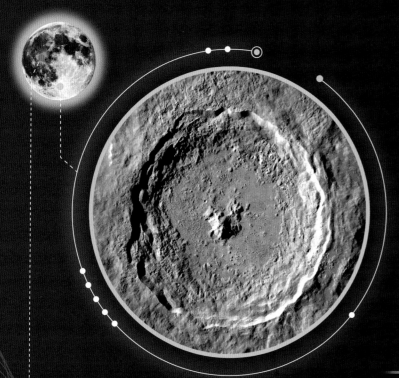

>>>>> TYCHO

When the moon is full, Tycho—with its rings and bright rays—can stand out in views of the lunar surface. Named after the Danish astronomer Tycho Brahe, it is one of the easiest craters to find on the moon. Measuring 53 miles (85 km) in diameter, Tycho is no more than 108 million years old, meaning it formed when dinosaurs were still roaming the Earth. It features a bright ray system that extends more than halfway around the moon.

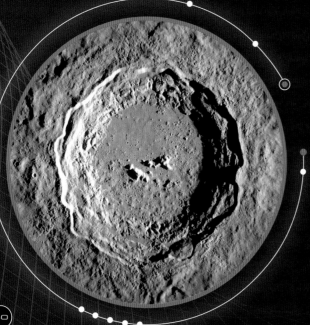

>>>>> COPERNICUS

Copernicus, nicknamed the "monarch of the moon," is a smaller impact crater. This young crater shows no lava flows on its floor, a sign of the crater's relatively recent formation. Named after astronomer Nicolaus Copernicus, the crater is about 58 miles (93 km) wide and 2.3 miles (3.7 km) deep. This sounds impressive until you put it into perspective. If the crater Copernicus were reduced down to the size of a nine-inch (23-cm) pie plate, it would be only one-third of an inch (8 mm) deep! Radiating out from Copernicus is a beautiful splash of dusty rays extending almost 500 miles (800 km) across the surrounding landscape.

Although most craters on the moon are billions of years old, new ones are still forming. Asteroids or space rocks traveling at 38,000 miles an hour (61,150 km/h) can slam into the moon at any time. On September 11, 2013, astronomers captured such an event on video. If you had been looking at the moon with your telescope that night, you might have seen this bright flash of light, too!

The
YOUNGEST
rocks on the moon
are as old as the
OLDEST
rocks on Earth.

As the Apollo 11 crew prepared to set down on the surface of the moon, they faced many great risks, including not having enough fuel to *land*! With less than 30 seconds of fuel supply remaining, and dust kicking up all around them, the long metal rods extending from the landing legs reached out to make contact with the lunar surface. Just in the nick of time, the courageous crew of the *Eagle* had landed!

WHAT THE APOLLO ASTRONAUTS DISCOVERED

STANDING ON THE MOON'S SURFACE, the Apollo astronauts found themselves in another world. With no atmosphere to pass along sound waves, it was silent. There was no weather, wind, or clouds. Overhead, the sun blazed brightly in the pitch-black sky.

On the moon, there is no twilight before nightfall, and there are no Earthrises or Earthsets. In fact, our home world never even moves across the lunar sky. It just hangs there in the same place, slowly undergoing phase changes.

Without an atmosphere, temperatures on the moon vary dramatically. Imagine moving around on a surface that can reach 273°F (134°C) in sunlight and minus 245°F (-154°C) in shade. This lack of atmosphere does stranger things, too. On Earth, the air in our atmosphere helps to spread out light, which allows it to illuminate things not in its direct path. Think of it this way: If you were to shine a flashlight straight at a wall in your darkened bedroom, you'd see a bright circle illuminated by the light. But you would also see areas surrounding it lit up by dimmer light diffused by the air. On the moon, with no air to scatter the light, all shadows appear pitch-black, making it impossible to tell what's hidden by them. Imagine stepping into a shallow hole that is really 30 feet (9 m) deep! What a surprise!

The Apollo astronauts found the moon a dusty place that smelled like wet ashes or gunpowder. Yet unlike Earth's smooth, weathered, and eroded dust, moondust is full of tiny, sharp rocks. These pieces were chipped off the lunar surface by micrometeorites hitting larger boulders. Each piece of dust is a spiky, barbed shard that could cause damage to your lungs if you were to accidentally breathe it in.

As dangerous as that sounds, lunar dust was crucial to one of Apollo's main missions: to learn how the moon formed. Comparing soil samples collected on the moon with samples from Earth, researchers found some similarities. Yet there were also enough differences to indicate that materials from other sources had been mixed in. This evidence proved that a collision between Earth and another object had created the moon! They also discovered that the youngest rocks on the moon are as old as the oldest rocks on Earth.

THERE ARE MANY INTERESTING PLACES

humans will explore in our solar system. Mars is a world that once had oceans, rivers, and streams beneath an atmosphere filled with white puffy clouds. Jupiter's moon Europa has vast oceans hidden beneath its icy surface. Saturn's moon Titan is like an ancient Earth, with a methane-rich orange atmosphere and icy seas covering its surface. So why bother exploring our moon, this lifeless, gray rock orbiting our planet?

With the looming threats of overpopulation, climate change, or a devastating disaster from space, our easy-to-reach neighbor may just help us survive.

Exploring the moon can prepare us to explore farther out into our solar neighborhood. As an example, voice communications between the moon and Earth travel faster than between Mars and Earth. On Earth, signals from Mars would take between 3 and 22 minutes, depending on the distances between the planets, just to travel one way. This means it might take over 40 minutes to say, "Hi, hello, how are you?" and get an answer back. From the moon, normal voice conversations to and from Earth could be carried on in real time.

The moon also has natural resources we could mine. Precious metals like magnesium,

hy bother
g our moon, this
ELESS,
Y ROCK
g our planet?

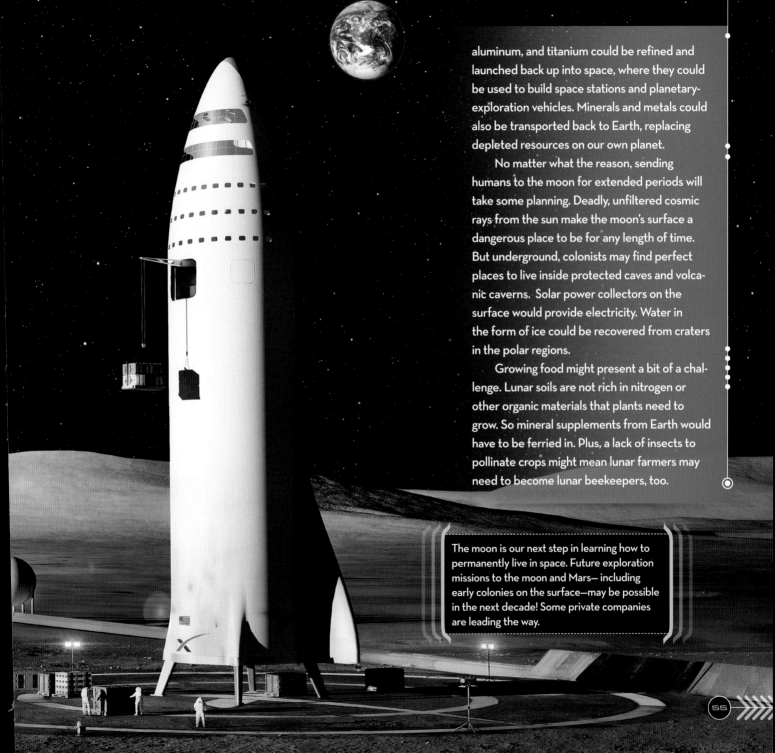

aluminum, and titanium could be refined and launched back up into space, where they could be used to build space stations and planetary-exploration vehicles. Minerals and metals could also be transported back to Earth, replacing depleted resources on our own planet.

No matter what the reason, sending humans to the moon for extended periods will take some planning. Deadly, unfiltered cosmic rays from the sun make the moon's surface a dangerous place to be for any length of time. But underground, colonists may find perfect places to live inside protected caves and volcanic caverns. Solar power collectors on the surface would provide electricity. Water in the form of ice could be recovered from craters in the polar regions.

Growing food might present a bit of a challenge. Lunar soils are not rich in nitrogen or other organic materials that plants need to grow. So mineral supplements from Earth would have to be ferried in. Plus, a lack of insects to pollinate crops might mean lunar farmers may need to become lunar beekeepers, too.

The moon is our next step in learning how to permanently live in space. Future exploration missions to the moon and Mars— including early colonies on the surface—may be possible in the next decade! Some private companies are leading the way.

Even now, countless NEW PLANETS ARE FORMING in our galaxy.

During the last days of our solar system, approximately four to five billion years in the future, the sun will exhaust its fuel supply. At that time, it will begin to expand outward, forming a red giant star. Its new size will engulf planets Mercury and Venus and push against the moon, ripping it apart, sending lunar debris back down onto the surface of Earth. Goodnight, moon!

ALL GOOD THINGS
MUST COME TO AN END

EVERYTHING IN THE UNIVERSE HAS A BEGINNING, A MIDDLE, AND AN END. Today, our sun is a middle-aged star. It has another four to five billion years to shine before it starts running out of hydrogen fuel and expands into a red giant. When that time comes, the sun may end up engulfing Mercury, Venus, Earth, and our moon.

Even if our planet isn't devoured, another possibility is that the sun's expanded atmosphere would create a drag on the moon, pushing it back in toward Earth. Eventually, our planet's stronger gravitational field would shred the moon to pieces. This small rubble would spread out, forming a spectacular Saturn-like ring once again around Earth. Within a few thousand years, the rubble would begin raining back down onto Earth's surface. If our planet survived this bombardment, it would spend the rest of its days traveling through space without its constant companion. This may seem like a sad ending to our moon, but the circle of "life" in the universe will go on.

Even now, countless new planets are forming in our Milky Way galaxy, many with wondrous moons racing around them. Do they look as beautiful as our moon does in our sky? Do life-forms on distant worlds tell stories about their moons, sing songs and write poetry about them, and venture out at night with small telescopes to explore them? Maybe so.

In the meantime, our moon is still here, lighting up our nighttime sky. We can still laugh as we try to imagine pictures of men and women, frogs and rabbits on its surface. We can gaze at it knowing someday some of us may walk on it again or make it our new home. This will be something few human beings have ever known before. Right there shining brightly in our skies is a world of "magnificent desolation": our magical stepping-stone to the planets and stars BEYOND!

MAKING THE MOON

Now it's time to get messy! We're going to make 3D models of lunar craters.

IN 1874, ONE OF THE MOST SOUGHT-AFTER BOOKS FEATURED PHOTOGRAPHS of plaster of paris models of the moon. The author was James Nasmyth, a Scottish amateur astronomer, telescope maker, entrepreneur, and space artist. His images turned out so real, many wondered if he had actually traveled to the moon! His beautiful plaster of paris models can still be viewed in the Science Museum of London.

CRATER CREATION

What you'll need:

>> An empty yogurt or cottage cheese container to mix the plaster in
>> Plaster of paris (see box below right)
>> Scissors
>> 2 sheets of letter-size printer paper
>> A black felt marker
>> A sheet of 1" (25 mm) thick pink or blue foam board cut into about a 12" (30 cm) square (a small pizza box will work, too)
>> Paper towels or paper napkins
>> A large water bucket to rinse out your mixing container and paintbrush
>> 2" (50 mm) wide masking tape
>> A spoon to stir and apply the plaster
>> A pencil with not too sharp a point and a rounded eraser (we will use this to make small craters)
>> A bottle of white glue; construction glue works best
>> An inexpensive 1" (25 mm) paintbrush
>> A small bag of gray grout or dry cement mix

HOW TO PREPARE PLASTER OF PARIS IN YOUR MIXING CONTAINER
What to do:
Pour half a cup (125 mL) of cold water into your empty mixing container. Take two large spoonfuls of dry plaster of paris and gently sprinkle them into the water. Stir the mixture around, and add a bit more plaster or water until it has the thickness of milk.

What to do:

1. First find a picture online of a crater that you want to make. The craters Tycho, Kepler, or Copernicus work well. Print two enlargements of the crater on letter-size paper. Cut one out and, using the black felt marker, trace it directly onto the foam board. Now we know how big our crater is going to be. The other printout will be our guide for adding details.

2. Prepare your plaster of paris. (See p. 58.)

3. Tear off little pieces of paper towel about 2" (50 mm) wide by 5–6" (125–150 mm) long. One at a time, dip them into the plaster and arrange them around the outline of the crater, squishing and shaping them with your fingers. Keep adding more plaster-soaked paper until the rim of the crater is complete. Work quickly because the plaster will set in about 6 to 10 minutes. Any plaster that drips onto the foam board can be smeared around using your fingers.

4. While waiting for your rim to harden, scrape out any extra plaster in the mixing container onto a newspaper and toss it into the trash. Rinse the mixing container in the bucket of water. Apply masking tape all around the outside edges of the foam board to keep plaster from running off the edges onto your surface.

5. Mix another full container of plaster.

6. Build the crater walls higher by dripping on spoonfuls of plaster, and spread some on the crater floor. Pour the new container of plaster around the outside of the crater to make the lunar surface higher. You may need to add another container of plaster later if the lunar surface is not high enough. Drip a little bit of plaster in the middle of the crater to make tiny peaks and wet the end of the pencil eraser and twist it around the drying plaster to make nice little craters. Use the sharp end of the pencil to trace in little cracks on the crater floor. Add more little craters as needed.

7. Clean out your mixing container once again, and set your crater aside in a warm room to let it dry overnight.

8. Now the real fun begins. In your clean mixing cup, pour in about a 1/2" (12 mm) layer of white glue and add about 1/2" (12 mm) of cold water to thin out the glue. Dip your paintbrush in the diluted glue and quickly paint over your entire plaster model with a layer of the glue.

9. Quickly sprinkle on the grout or cement mix until everything is covered. Now, once again, wait until everything dries. Then, pick up the foam board, walk outside and gently blow off any loose dust.

10. There you have it! You have just made your own model of a lunar crater. If you want to get really crafty, put your model in a darkened room and shine a light on it from one direction, just as the sun would be shining on the moon. With a cell phone, take a picture of it. It will look like you shot a close-up image of the moon through a big telescope!

IF YOU CANNOT FIND PLASTER OF PARIS, YOU CAN ALSO USE PAPIER-MÂCHÉ.

What you'll need:

- ›› 1/2 cup white glue
- ›› 1/2 cup water
- ›› Newspaper torn into 1" x 6" (25 x 150 mm) pieces
- ›› Your mixing container
- ›› Gray poster or acrylic paint

What to do:

- ›› Mix the glue and water together until smooth.
- ›› Follow step 1 from above.
- ›› Make your rim as in step 3 above.
- ›› Dip pieces of newspaper into the glue mixture and layer them over the rim, adding up to four layers for strength. Flatten the layers with your fingers so the edges blend together.
- ›› When dry, paint your crater with gray poster or acrylic paint.

EXPLORATION GUIDE

THE MOON IS THE PRIME TARGET FOR ALL BEGINNING OBSERVERS because it's easy to find and shows a wealth of detail in the smallest of instruments. All you need is a small telescope, three to eight inches (80-200 mm) in aperture, and the map on page 39 to guide you along your journey. So grab your telescope! It's time to explore the moon.

Best Viewing Checklist

>> When the moon is high in the sky
>> During the first 14 days of the moon's cycle
>> In an area that doesn't have many bright lights

Magnification

>> Always begin your observations using a low-power magnification. Make sure the entire moon is visible in the eyepiece.
>> Sweeping across the lunar landscape at 60x to 100x power, mountain ranges, vast lava plains, and magnificent craters come into view.

When to Explore

Following the lunar cycle will help you know what you'll be able to explore—and when. The new moon phase starts the cycle at Day 1 in the lunar phase calendar. By Day 14 the moon has grown to its full phase. These 14 days are the best time for viewing. In the 14 days following the full moon phase, the moon rises too late in the evening (or early morning hours) to be easily observed—especially if you are going to school the next day!

Here are the different phases and days when the top 10 sites on the moon (see pages 39-51) are best viewed:

DAY 5	DAY 7	DAY 12	DAY 13	DAY 14

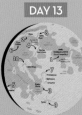

FOR CENTURIES, THE ONLY WAY TO RECORD SURFACE FEATURES on the moon was by making drawings. Sketching the changing faces of the moon today can still be fun. It also teaches us where lunar features are located and the best times to see them. To become a genuine lunar artist, let's go outside and sketch.

What you'll need:

- » A comfortable chair or box to sit on while looking through the eyepiece of your telescope. It's harder to draw when standing up.
- » A small telescope to be used at about 50x to 60x magnification
- » A handheld clipboard
- » A No. 2 pencil
- » A flashlight or headlamp to illuminate your drawings as you work
- » A piece of letter-size white paper to draw on
- » A round object about 4 to 6 inches (10–15 cm) in diameter, such as an empty yogurt container or a small paint can.

What to do:

1. Place the round object in the middle of your paper and trace around it with your pencil. That's the outline of the moon that you are now going to fill in.

2. The first thing to draw in is the terminator line. Remember, that's the dividing line between night and day on the moon. Everything you draw in will be on the daytime side.

3. Look through your telescope and lightly sketch everything you see on the daytime side of the terminator.

4. When you're done, go back inside and make the lines darker. Also shadow in the nighttime area. In the upper left corner of the paper, be sure to write the date of your drawing, the time of night, and the power of the eyepiece you used on your telescope. Go outside on several nights and make a drawing each night. You will be amazed at how lunar features change and how the moon becomes much more familiar!

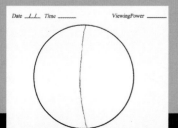

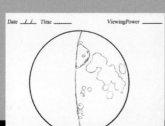

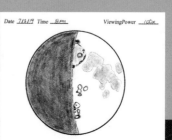

Boldface indicates illustrations.

Check out David A. Aguilar's other books!

13 Planets, National Geographic Kids

Alien Worlds, National Geographic Kids

Cosmic Catastrophes, Smithsonian/Viking
Books for Young Readers

Seven Wonders of the Milky Way, Smithsonian/
Viking Books for Young Readers

Seven Wonders of the Solar System,
Smithsonian/Viking Books for Young Readers

Space Encyclopedia, National Geographic Kids

Super Stars, National Geographic Kids

Where to Go to Look Through a Telescope
Ask an adult to help you search online for local
astronomy clubs, planetariums, and science centers that hold public viewing nights. There's likely
one near you! Also contact your local library—
some may have telescopes you can check out for
a couple of weeks just like a book!

Where to Go to Use a Remote Telescope
Try MicroObservatory, a wonderful Harvard/
NASA website where you can control a remote
telescope, take images with it, and do great
projects and activities, all online!

mo-www.harvard.edu/OWN

And be sure to visit my author's page for astronomy updates, new books coming out, and my
latest outer space artwork.

davidaguilar.org

Tips for Choosing a First Telescope
backyardastronomy.com/Backyard_Astronomy/
The_Best_Beginner_Telescopes.html

skyandtelescope.com/astronomy-equipment/
how-to-choose-a-telescope

space.com/29798-best-telescopes-for-kids.html

For Adults
Check out these sites to help your kids choose the telescope that's right for them.

Cloudynights classifieds for great used telescopes
cloudynights.com/classifieds

Orion telescopes
telescope.com

CREDITS

All artwork, illustrations, and photography by David A. Aguilar, unless noted here: pages 42, 45, 49, 50: NASA; pages 54-55, SpaceX with author modifications

---

ANSWER TO PAGE 19
What's odd about this image?
It looks like a daytime image, but look closer—there are stars in the sky! Believe it or not, this 30-second exposure was taken at midnight with a full moon overhead. Sunlight reflecting off the surface of the moon turned night on Earth into day.

I sincerely want to thank my resourceful and imaginative editor, Shelby Alinsky Lees, creative art director Amanda Larsen, and spot-on image researcher Sarah J. Mock and cartographer Michael McNey for their fantastic teamwork in bringing this beautiful book on the moon to life! A shimmering box of moonbeams also goes out to my wife, the amazing Ms. Astrid, for her thoughtful insights, playful humor, and never- ending assistance in making *LUNA* rise above the distant mountains and shine! This book is also dedicated to my space amigos, Tim Abbott, Gary Andrijasevich, Alec Palao, and Derek See. Lastly, this book is for all you young readers, including Isaac and Ryan Walker, who can't wait to start viewing craters on the moon, the rings of Saturn, and the magnificent universe beyond. Be bold, young space cadets—get out there and explore! —DAA

Text copyright © 2019 David A. Aguilar
Illustrations copyright © 2019 National Geographic Partners, LLC
Compilation copyright © 2019 National Geographic Partners, LLC

Published by National Geographic Partners, LLC. All rights reserved. Reproduction of the whole or any part of the contents without written permission from the publisher is prohibited.

Since 1888, the National Geographic Society has funded more than 12,000 research, exploration, and preservation projects around the world. The Society receives funds from National Geographic Partners, LLC, funded in part by your purchase. A portion of the proceeds from this book supports this vital work. To learn more, visit natgeo.com/info.

NATIONAL GEOGRAPHIC and Yellow Border Design are trademarks of the National Geographic Society, used under license.

For more information, visit national geographic.com, call 1-800-647-5463, or write to the following address:

National Geographic Partners
1145 17th Street N.W.
Washington, D.C. 20036-4688 U.S.A.

Visit us online at nationalgeographic.com/books

For librarians and teachers:
ngchildrensbooks.org

More for kids from National Geographic:
natgeokids.com

National Geographic Kids magazine inspires children to explore their world with fun yet educational articles on animals, science, nature, and more. Using fresh storytelling and amazing photography, *Nat Geo Kids* shows kids ages 6 to 14 the fascinating truth about the world—and why they should care. kids.nationalgeographic.com/subscribe

For information about special discounts for bulk purchases, please contact National Geographic Books Special Sales: specialsales @natgeo.com

For rights or permissions inquiries, please contact National Geographic Books Subsidiary Rights: bookrights @natgeo.com

Designed by Amanda Larsen

Hardcover ISBN: 978-1-4263-3322-4
Reinforced library binding ISBN: 978-1-4263-3323-1

Printed in China
18/PPS/1

Two carved statues guarding the Greek Temple of Diana gaze out into space as Jules Verne's 1865 spaceship arrives at the moon. After completing their mission on the lunar surface, Verne's returning astronauts landed in the ocean, where a ship picked them up, just as the Apollo missions did 104 years later.